Why is this Book Cover Different?

This is one of three books on which we have recently
changed the covers in order to promote
the concept that this
Bible Study Series is about:

The Intriguing Lives of Obscure Bible Characters!

Unfortunately our initial covers didn't send
this message, so we are experimenting
to see if these new covers do send
the right message about these books.

The OBSCURE BIBLE STUDY SERIES is a 9 book series
based on unique, uncommon, and even obscure
Bible characters and events.

"Wisdom That Transforms. Action That Lasts."

The Get Wisdom Commitment

At Get Wisdom Publishing we believe that true wisdom has the power to transform lives. Our mission is to equip readers with timeless insights and practical tools that inspire growth, guide decisions, and empower purposeful living. We don't just inform—we empower.

Our books combine profound understanding with real-life application, enabling readers to unlock their potential and navigate life's challenges with clarity and confidence. With each step guided by wisdom, we help you create lasting change and live the life you deserve.

When wisdom meets purpose, transformation follows.

The *OBSCURE* Bible Study Series

Grow in your faith through investigating
unusual and obscure biblical characters.

*"Deep Biblical Wisdom.
Real-Life Faith Application."*

The OBSCURE Bible Study Journey

Miracles
&
Rebellion

The good, the bad, and the indifferent.

Personal Study Guide
Book 7

Deepen Your Faith.

Stephen H Berkey

GETWISDOM
PUBLISHING

COPYRIGHT

ISBN 978-1-952359-14-9   (Leader Guide, paperback)

ISBN 978-1-952359-15-6   (Leader Guide, ebook)

ISBN 978-1-952359-16-3   (Personal Study Guide, paperback)

ISBN 978-1-952359-17-0   (Personal Study Guide, ebook)

Audiobook available   (amazon.com and audible.com)

Bible Translations Used:

Unmarked scriptures and scriptures marked ESV are taken from THE HOLY BIBLE, ENGLISH STANDARD VERSION (ESV): Scriptures taken from THE HOLY BIBLE, ENGLISH STANDARD VERSION ® Copyright© 2001 by Crossway, a publishing ministry of Good News Publishers. Used by permission.

Scriptures marked NIV are taken from the NEW INTERNATIONAL VERSION (NIV): Scripture taken from THE HOLY BIBLE, NEW INTERNATIONAL VERSION ®. Copyright© 1973, 1978, 1984, 2011 by Biblica, Inc.™. Used by permission of Zondervan.

Scriptures marked HCSB are taken from the HOLMAN CHRISTIAN STANDARD BIBLE (HCSB): Scripture taken from the HOLMAN CHRISTIAN STANDARD BIBLE, copyright© 1999, 2000, 2002, 2003 by Holman Bible Publishers, Nashville Tennessee. All rights reserved.

Discover the biblical characters that mainstream studies forget – and the timeless lessons they teach."

TABLE OF CONTENTS

CONTENTS

FREE PDF RESOURCES

Living Wisely
The Life Planning Guide

A Quick-Start Guide to Purposeful Living and Wise Decisions!

Discover the five life domains: purpose, people, principles, productivity, and perspective. Wisdom is the ability to apply truth and logic to real-life decisions and produce good outcomes. It influences your choices and will produce action that lasts. Consider and apply the five practical wisdom principles for daily living. (6 pages)

Free PDF: https://getwisdompublishing.com/resource-registration/

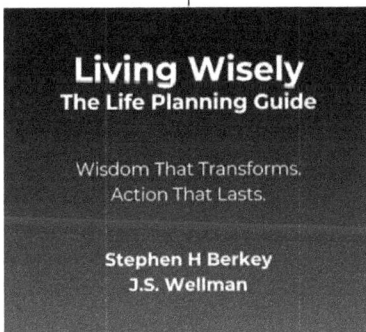

Living Wisely
The Life Planning Guide

Wisdom That Transforms.
Action That Lasts.

Stephen H Berkey
J.S. Wellman

Free PDF

Five Practical Principles For Life

When wisdom meets purpose, transformation follows.

Free PDF
Wise Decision-Making
[Get the ebook version for 99 cents]

You can make good choices.

This free resource provides a project-oriented perspective and gives ten detailed steps to analyze issues/problems to determine a solution. (26 pages)

Good decisions expand your horizons. Don't allow the fear of decision-making paralyze your ability to make good choices. Think through the reasonable alternatives and move forward. When your eyes are on the goal, making good decisions is easier.

Free PDF: https://getwisdompublishing.com/resource-registration/

Kindle ebook for 99 cents: https://www.amazon.com/dp/B09SYGWRVL/

Ebook

Free PDF

Make Thoughtful Decisions!

Good decisions expand your horizons.

Why Study OBSCURE Characters?

Unique, New, and Fresh
For experienced Bible students these characters will provide a fresh and interesting approach to Bible study. Since most of the material will be unfamiliar to the participants, new believers or those just starting Bible study should not feel intimidated by students who have been studying for years. Most readers will not be acquainted with the majority of the characters and events in this series.

Knowledge of Scripture
These studies are a great introduction for those just beginning Bible study. Regardless of their level of knowledge, everyone should find the characters and stories provide an opportunity to grow in their faith through investigating fascinating and unusual biblical stories and incidents.

Valuable Life Lessons
These lesser-known characters are a lot like you and me. God uses all sorts of people to accomplish His plans! You will become familiar with ordinary people, strange characters, and people living on the fringe of life who have the same troubles and challenges as people today. The deep truths and life lessons embedded in these studies should be valuable. They will provide new insights to scripture.

*"Unlock Biblical Wisdom.
Transform Your faith!"*

ABOUT THE LEADER GUIDE

All of the books in this Bible Study series have an extensive Leader Guide. If you are a participant in a group, a Leader Guide is not necessary, unless you want the author's answers. If you are studying independently, you may want the Leader Guide.

In the Guide the answers follow the questions with a small amount of space for the Leader's personal responses. If you are using the Leader Guide and want to do the study without the influence of the author's answers the best solution is to obtain the blank Worksheets, which are free. This will allow you to record your answers separately before reviewing the answers in the Leader Guide.

See the instructions on the previous "FREE RESOURCES" page to access the free Worksheets.

"Discover the Overlooked.
Apply it to Your Life!"

Book Description

Challenge Your Faith: Provocative Truths from Unexpected Sources

Are you weary of surface-level answers? Do you dare to wrestle with the challenging aspects of faith, even when it's uncomfortable?

"Miracles & Rebellion" isn't for the faint of heart. If you're struggling with unanswered prayers or the persistent pull of temptation, this book offers a fresh, honest look at those moments when faith feels strained to its breaking point. These are names you may not know, like Aeneas, a paralytic man that Peter heals, and the Blind man, whose life Jesus changed. Are you ready to be one?

Through focused biblical wisdom and relatable stories, this study will guide you on a journey of self-discovery and spiritual renewal. Dig deeper into the lives of Korah, whose rebellion shook the foundations of Israel, and Haman, whose treachery led to his own demise. Learn to recognize the subtle temptations that can derail your faith and discover how to stand firm in the face of adversity.

This is more than just a Bible study. It's an invitation to wrestle with provocative truths, rediscover the power of faith, and unlock a renewed passion for the journey ahead.

Transform your understanding of Scripture. Your path to deeper wisdom awaits!

Book 7 contrasts the stories of biblical characters who rebelled against God with those who trusted, believed, and had great faith. In the first lesson Korah a dissatisfied Levite, rebelled against Moses and Aaron during the forty years the Israelites wandered in the wilderness. Rebellion is an ugly business, particularly when the adversary is the Lord God! The second lesson features another character with an evil disposition: Haman, Queen Esther's antagonist. We then move to The Gospel of John who describes only eight miracles of Jesus and one of them is the healing of a blind man near the Pool of Siloam. This miracle was additional proof that Jesus was the Messiah.

In Acts 9 we find another similar miracle when Aeneas was raised from the dead by Peter at Lydda, a small community 25 miles northwest of Jerusalem. Interestingly the text says nothing about Aeneas asking to be healed, the extent of his faith, or what he did after he was raised from the dead. But, "all the residents . . . saw him, and they turned to the Lord!"

Shadrach, Meshack, and Abednigo demonstrate amazing trust in God in their journey through the fiery furnace, providing us with an example of those who are totally committed to their God, no matter what the consequences. Alexander, the coppersmith, is a lesson about a rebellious character who created problems for Paul. He along with Hymenaeus, whom we studied in Book 2 of this series, were accused of blasphemy, and Paul said they were "handed over to Satan."

Next we investigate the circumstances of the Slave Girl with the ability to predict the future and we end with Paul healing a crippled man at Lystra. The local people thought Paul and Barnabas were Greek gods. The celebration of a healing didn't last long because some unhappy and unbelieving Jews created a firestorm of protest against Paul and Barnabas, and outsiders came from Antioch and Iconium, stoned Paul, and dragged him out of the city.

"Scripture holds answers in unexpected places. Our unique Bible studies reveal overlooked wisdom for today's challenges."

INTRODUCTION

*We equip readers with timeless wisdom and practical tools
that transform, not just inform. Our books combine
deep insights with real-life application
to create lasting change.*

Description of The OBSCURE Bible Study Series

This unique series uses a number of lesser-known Bible characters
and events to explore such major themes as Angels, being Born
Again, Courage, Death, Evangelism, Faithfulness, Forgiveness,
Grace, Hell, Leadership, Miracles, the Remnant, the Sabbath,
Salvation, Rebellion, Sovereignty, Thankfulness, Women, the
World, Creation, and End Times.

The series as a whole provides both a broad and fresh
understanding of the nature of God as we see Him act in the lives
of people we've never examined before.

Most of the people chosen for these studies are unfamiliar because
they are mentioned only a few times in Scripture – fifteen only
once or twice. Others, although more familiar, are included
because of their particular contribution to kingdom work.

For example, Scripture mentions Shamgar only twice. One verse in
Judges 3:31 tells his story and 5:6 simply establishes a timeline and
says nothing more about him. Then there is Nicodemus, with
whom we associate the concept of being "born again." His name
appears only 5 times, all in one short passage in the book of John.
Eve, although obviously not obscure, is included in order to
investigate the creation story.

Group Discussion or Individual Study

These studies can be done individually or in a small discussion
group. The real value of the study is in the discussion questions.
We all see life differently and the thoughts and ideas shared in a
group will often lead to a richer understanding of the Scripture. The

questions often require the participant to put himself (herself) in the mind or circumstances of that person in the Scriptures.

The commentary portion of the introductory material in each lesson is there to help clarify the passage and set the stage for the discussion questions. The questions are designed to help the student understand the meaning of the text itself and explore the kingdom implications from a personal point of view.

Ideal For Both New and Mature Bible Students

These lessons have three underlying questions:

- "Who is this person?"
- "What is happening here?"
- "What is the implication for my life?"

Because of the obscurity of the characters under study, chances are that even experienced participants with prior understanding of the lesson's theme will find fresh material to explore. Both new and long-time students will be challenged by the life lessons these unfamiliar characters can teach them.

Format of Lessons

Each lesson begins with the Scripture using the ESV translation followed by short sections titled "Context," "What Do We Know," and "Observations." The discussion questions are designed to help the student understand the subject and are followed by several application questions.

"We believe applied wisdom empowers life change. Our books provide clarity, inspiration, and tools to equip readers to live their best life."

Korah
the rebellious Levite

Occurrences of "Korah" in the Bible: 12

Theme: Rebellion

Scripture

Numbers 16   Korah's Rebellion

Now Korah the son of Izhar, son of Kohath, son of Levi, and Dathan and Abiram the sons of Eliab, and On the son of Peleth, sons of Reuben, took men. 2 And they rose up before Moses, with a number of the people of Israel, 250 chiefs of the congregation, chosen from the assembly, well-known men. 3 They assembled themselves together against Moses and against Aaron and said to them, "You have gone too far! For all in the congregation are holy, every one of them, and the Lord is among them. Why then do you exalt yourselves above the assembly of the Lord?" 4 When Moses heard it, he fell on his face, 5 and he said to Korah and all his company, "In the morning the Lord will show who is his, and who is holy, and will bring him near to him. The one whom he chooses he will bring near to him. 6 Do this: take censers, Korah and all his company;

7 put fire in them and put incense on them before the Lord tomorrow, and the man whom the Lord chooses shall be the holy one. You have gone too far, sons of Levi!" 8 And Moses said to Korah, "Hear now, you sons of Levi: 9 is it too small a thing for you that the God of Israel has separated you from the congregation of Israel, to bring you near to himself, to do service in the tabernacle of the Lord and to stand before the congregation to minister to them, 10 and that he has brought you near him, and all your brothers the sons of Levi with you? And would you seek the priesthood also? 11 Therefore it is against the Lord that you and all your company have gathered together. What is Aaron that you grumble against him?"

12 And Moses sent to call Dathan and Abiram the sons of Eliab, and they said, "We will not come up. 13 Is it a small thing that you have brought us up out of a land flowing with milk and honey, to kill us in the wilderness, that you must also make yourself a prince over us? 14 Moreover, you have not brought us into a land flowing with milk and honey, nor given us inheritance of fields and vineyards. Will you put out the eyes of these men? We will not come up." 15 And Moses was very angry and said to the Lord, "Do not respect their offering. I have not taken one donkey from them, and I have not harmed one of them."

16 And Moses said to Korah, "Be present, you and all your company, before the Lord, you and they, and Aaron, tomorrow. 17 And let every one of you take his censer and put incense on it, and every one of you bring before the Lord his censer, 250 censers; you also, and Aaron, each his censer." 18 So every man took his censer and put fire in them and laid incense on them and stood at the entrance of the tent of meeting with Moses and Aaron. 19 Then Korah assembled all the congregation against them at the entrance of the tent of meeting. And the glory of the Lord appeared to all the congregation.

20 And the Lord spoke to Moses and to Aaron, saying, 21 "Separate yourselves from among this congregation, that I may consume them in a moment." 22 And they fell on their faces and said, "O God, the God of the spirits of all flesh, shall one man sin, and will you be angry with all the congregation?" 23 And the Lord spoke to Moses, saying, 24 "Say to the congregation, Get away from the dwelling of Korah, Dathan, and Abiram."

. . . 31 And as soon as he had finished speaking all these words, the ground under them split apart. 32 And the earth opened its mouth and swallowed them up, with their households and all the people who belonged to Korah and all their goods. 33 So they and all that belonged to them went down alive into Sheol, and the earth closed over them, and they perished from the midst of the assembly. 34 And all Israel who were around them fled at their cry, for they said, "Lest the earth swallow us up!" 35 And fire came out from the Lord and consumed the 250 men offering the incense.

36 Then the Lord spoke to Moses, saying, 37 "Tell Eleazar the son of Aaron the priest to take up the censers out of the blaze. Then scatter the fire far and wide, for they have become holy. 38 As for the censers of these men who have sinned at the cost of their lives, let them be made into hammered plates as a covering for the altar, for they offered them before the Lord, and they became holy. Thus they shall be a sign to the people of Israel." . . .

41 But on the next day all the congregation of the people of Israel grumbled against Moses and against Aaron, saying, "You have killed the people of the Lord." 42 And when the congregation had assembled against Moses and against Aaron, they turned toward the tent of meeting. And behold, the cloud covered it, and the glory of the Lord appeared. 43 And Moses and Aaron came to the front of the tent of meeting, 44 and the Lord spoke to Moses, saying, 45 "Get away from the midst of this congregation, that I may consume them in a moment." And they fell on their faces. 46 And Moses said to Aaron, "Take your censer, and put fire on it from off the altar and lay incense on it and carry it quickly to the congregation and make atonement for them, for wrath has gone out from the Lord; the plague has begun." 47 So Aaron took it as Moses said and ran into the midst of the assembly. And behold, the plague had already begun among the people. And he put on the incense and made atonement for the people. 48 And he stood between the dead and the living, and the plague was stopped. 49 Now those who died in the plague were 14,700, besides those who died in the affair of Korah. 50 And Aaron returned to Moses at the entrance of the tent of meeting, when the plague was stopped. ESV

The Context

For 400 years the children of Israel had been enslaved in Egypt and then God sent Moses to rescue them. They escaped Egypt by the miracle of the Red Sea and reached Mt. Sinai where they were given the Law. But they rebelled and refused to trust in the Lord so He sentenced them to wander in the wilderness for 40 years. The timeframe of this story is somewhere near the middle of that 40 year period. Thus, all the adults in this story had been eyewitnesses to the miracles that God had performed in bringing them out of Egyptian slavery and caring for them in the wilderness.

The Levites, one of the twelve tribes, were devoted to serving God as priests and as servants in worship. Because this was their full-time work, all the other tribes contributed tithes and offerings to support them and their work for God. Korah was a Levite. Because of his status as a Levite, he would be privileged. But Korah and his friends were not satisfied. They wanted more, and because of their dissatisfaction, they rebelled against Moses and Aaron.

What Do We Know?

What is "rebellion"? Webster says that *to rebel* means "to change or remove those in authority; to oppose openly those in authority; to refuse to obey normal rules and standards; or to defy or resist those in established government positions." The word is often used to represent insurgence, insurrection, mutiny, or revolt.

This passage describes Korah's rebellion. The words rebel, rebelled, or rebellion appear in the Bible more than 120 times. This characteristic of the human spirit is an ugly reminder that when we don't get what we want, or if we are not pleased with our station in life, then we rebel. We think we will be happy if we take control. God help us!

The problem is that God takes personally any attempt to rebel against His plans and purposes – that's why the Israelites were wandering around the desert in the first place! Moses, as the appointed leader, was the only one allowed into God's presence. Moses had met and spoken with God on the mountain. He was the leader of the people as God led them from one spot in the wilderness to another.

We probably should not be surprised that Korah wasn't happy. The Israelites as a whole had been grumbling about something ever since they had left Egypt. They had been moved around the desert wilderness with nothing to do but eat manna and quail and grumble!

Korah thought he and his friends deserved a better leader. Ironically Moses hadn't really wanted to be the leader in the first place. Remember how he made excuses to get out of the job of confronting Pharaoh and leading the people out of Egypt? Korah and his band of traitors had so poisoned the minds of the people that even after the Lord destroyed him and all 250 men, the people returned the next day grumbling against Moses.

Implications and Observations

Rebellion is very destructive and the consequences seldom work out well for anybody involved. That's especially true when the adversary is the Lord God! In western society today the underdog who rebels against authority is often portrayed as the hero. He exerts his rights against authority and always wins at the end of the story. Society often tends to elevate his plight and give him credit, regardless of whether his cause is just or unjust. Today someone who is unhappy often feels he is entitled to do whatever is necessary to make his situation acceptable to himself, regardless of the consequences. But make no mistake about it: God hates rebellion!

Note in the text who did all the praying. Only Moses and Aaron prayed! True servant leaders put the needs of others ahead of their own. Three times in this chapter (16:4, 22, 45) Moses fell on his face in prayer. It is instructive to recognize that prayer was the first thing that Moses did when he was confronted with Korah and the rebellion.

"Undoing the Damage"

There is a story of a boy who was constantly *rebelling* against his father. This boy was destroying his own life by his *rebellion*, but he refused to heed his father's words. One day, the dad said to the boy, "I want to show you what you're doing to your life. I'm going to put a wooden post in our front yard. Every time you rebel, I will put a nail in this post. Every time you obey, I will pull out one nail." The boy's first thought was, "I'm going to do everything I can to fill that post with nails." And he did.

In two months' time, he filled the post with nails. But he also began to feel the damage he was doing to his own life and to his parents' lives. With true remorse, the boy began to obey his father. One by one, the nails came out. When the last nail came out of the post, the boy broke down in tears. The dad asked, "Son, why are you crying?" And the boy replied, "I got rid of the nails, but I can't get rid of the holes."[1]

This story identifies one of the biggest problems with rebellion. Actions always have consequences, and the impact and result of rebellion cannot always be repaired (the hole in this story). One can patch the hole, but that is only an external solution – the original wood that comprised the area where the hole was can never be restored. It can be repaired, but not restored to its original form.

Discussion Questions

A. GENERAL

A1. How many died in this story?

A2. If you had been one of the innocent people in the community at that time, what would you have been thinking at the end of the first day?

A3. If you examined movies, TV dramas, books, documentaries, etc., how is the one who rebels against authority often treated?

        Q. What can this produce?

A4. Find an example in the Bible when someone or some group rebelled against authority. What happened? What, if anything, did God do?

A5. Who were the people who came with Korah (16:2) and how did they come (16:3)?

A6. Nu 16:3 also says that the rebels claimed that the whole community was holy (set apart) and the Lord was with them. Is there any truth to that statement?

A7. Who appointed Moses and Aaron?

       Q. Who wanted to appoint the new leaders?

A8. <u>Who</u> specifically was Korah rebelling against, and what do you think he <u>wants</u> to achieve?

      <u>WHO</u>

      <u>WANT</u>

A9. Do you think that Aaron could have retained the priesthood if Moses had been removed?

A10. List the actions of Dathan and Abiram in 16:12-14.

      1) Refused to meet with _____.

      2) Mocked Moses: "bring us from Egypt to _____ us in wilderness."

3) Accused Moses of responsibility for their wilderness __
_____ against the people.

4) Accused Moses of appointing himself as _____.

5) Blamed Moses for Israel not possessing _____.

6) Re-stated their disobedience – "we will _____ come."

A11. How would you compare Korah's situation to the New Testament story of the Prodigal Son?

A12. How would you compare this story to the making of a golden calf at Horeb? (Ex 32:1-11; Dt 9:7-8)

Golden Calf vs *Korah*

WHO:

LEADERS:

EGYPT:

DESTRUCTION:

PRAYER:

RESULT:

A13. Do you think the Israelites had any legitimate reason to grumble? If so, why? If not, then why would they grumble the day after God destroyed Korah and his followers?

Q. Who was leading the grumbling on the day after Korah was destroyed?

A14. This might be described as a horror story because there were innocent women and children destroyed. Would that be a good description?

A15. Why did God want them to create a covering for the altar out of the dead rebel's firepans (16:38)?

Q. In 16:36 how did the firepans become holy?

A16. What significance might you assign to 16:48? How would you explain the significance?
Numbers 16:48   *And he stood between the dead and the living, and the plague was stopped.* ESV

A17. Why do you think that God reacted so dramatically in this situation to Korah's rebellion?

A18. What lesson(s) should we learn from this story?

A19. What do we learn about God in this story?

B. APPLICATION

B1. In similar circumstances, would prayer be your first reaction? What would you have done? What would you have prayed for?

B2. Do you think it is acceptable to rebel against authority to accomplish what <u>you</u> think is right? Explain.

B3. In our society, who would we blame for Korah's actions?

B4. If you wanted to ensure that situations like this do not occur, what would you do?

B5. Are you pushing the envelope of disobedience with God in any way? Has He given you a warning?

THE GOOD NEWS:

Lamentations 3:31-33   *For the Lord will not cast off forever, 32 but, though he cause grief, he will have compassion according to the abundance of his steadfast love; 33 for he does not willingly afflict or grieve the children of men.* ESV

Haman & Zeresh
Queen Esther's antagonists

Occurrences of "Haman/Zeresh" in the Bible: 46/4

Themes: Treachery; Trusted Advisors

Note: Zeresh appears only in chapters 5-6 of Esther while Haman is a prominent character throughout the book. We will restrict this study primarily to chapters 5-6 in order to observe how Zeresh influenced Haman.

Scripture

Esther 3:2-6

And all the king's servants who were at the king's gate bowed down and paid homage to Haman, for the king had so commanded concerning him. But Mordecai did not bow down or pay homage. 3 Then the king's servants who were at the king's gate said to Mordecai, "Why do you transgress the king's command?" 4 And when they spoke to him day after day and he would not listen to them, they told Haman, in order to see whether Mordecai's words would stand, for he had told them that he was a Jew. 5 And when Haman saw that Mordecai did not bow down or pay homage to him, Haman was filled with fury. 6 But he disdained to lay hands on Mordecai alone. So, as they had made known to him the people of Mordecai, Haman sought to destroy all the Jews, the people of Mordecai, throughout the whole kingdom of Ahasuerus. ESV

NOTE: If you are not familiar with Esther's whole story, it might be very helpful to read the entire book of Esther before starting this study. There are only ten chapters, it's a quick read, and it's an exciting story.

Esther 5:9-6:14   Haman Plans to Hang Mordecai

And Haman went out that day joyful and glad of heart. But when Haman saw Mordecai in the king's gate, that he neither rose nor trembled before him, he was filled with wrath against Mordecai. 10 Nevertheless, Haman restrained himself and went home, and he sent and brought his friends and his wife Zeresh. 11 And Haman recounted to them the splendor of his riches, the number of his sons, all the promotions with which the king had honored him, and how he had advanced him above the officials and the servants of the king. 12 Then Haman said, "Even Queen Esther let no one but me come with the king to the feast she prepared. And tomorrow also I am invited by her together with the king. 13 Yet all this is worth nothing to me, so long as I see Mordecai the Jew sitting at the king's gate." 14 Then his wife Zeresh and all his friends said to him, "Let a gallows fifty cubits high be made, and in the morning tell the king to have Mordecai hanged upon it. Then go joyfully with the king to the feast." This idea pleased Haman, and he had the gallows made.

The King Honors Mordecai

6 On that night the king could not sleep. And he gave orders to bring the book of memorable deeds, the chronicles, and they were read before the king. 2 And it was found written how Mordecai had told about Bigthana and Teresh, two of the king's eunuchs, who guarded the threshold, and who had sought to lay hands on King Ahasuerus. 3 And the king said, "What honor or distinction has been bestowed on Mordecai for this?" The king's young men who attended him said, "Nothing has been done for him." 4 And the king said, "Who is in the court?" Now Haman had just entered the outer court of the king's palace to speak to the king about having Mordecai hanged on the gallows that he had prepared for him. 5 And the king's young men told him, "Haman is there, standing in the court." And the king said, "Let him come in." 6 So Haman came in, and the king said to him, "What should be done to the man whom the king delights to honor?" And Haman said to himself, "Whom would the king delight to honor more than me?" 7 And Haman said to the king, "For the man whom the king delights to honor, 8 let royal robes be brought, which the king has worn, and the horse that the king has ridden, and on whose head a royal crown is set. 9 And let the robes and the horse be handed over to one of the king's most noble officials. Let them dress the man whom the king delights to honor, and let them lead him on the horse through the square of the city, proclaiming before him: 'Thus shall it be done to the man whom the king delights to honor.'" 10 Then the king said to Haman, "Hurry; take the robes and the horse, as you have said, and do so to Mordecai the Jew who sits at the king's gate. Leave out nothing that you have mentioned." 11 So Haman took the robes and the horse, and he dressed Mordecai and led him through the square of the city, proclaiming before him, "Thus shall it be done to the man whom the king delights to honor."

12 Then Mordecai returned to the king's gate. But Haman hurried to his house, mourning and with his head covered. 13 And Haman told his wife Zeresh and all his friends everything that had happened to him. Then his wise men and his wife Zeresh said to him, "If Mordecai, before whom you have begun to fall, is of the Jewish people, you will not overcome him but will surely fall before him."

Esther Reveals Haman's Plot
14 While they were yet talking with him, the king's eunuchs arrived and hurried to bring Haman to the feast that Esther had prepared.
ESV

The Context

In Chapter 2 we learned that Mordecai had discovered a plot to kill King Ahasuerus. He reported the plot to Queen Esther who in turn told the king what Mordecai had reported, and the plot was foiled. After this the king found reason to elevate one of his officials named Haman, giving him a seat above all the other officials. But

Mordacai, Queen Esther's adoptive father, was a Jew like the Queen, and would not bow down and pay homage to Haman (3:2). This enraged Haman and he developed a plan to destroy all the Jewish people in the kingdom.

Orders to annihilate all the Jews were written and sent to all the provinces.

> Esther 4:1   *When Mordecai learned all that had been done, Mordecai tore his clothes and put on sackcloth and ashes, and went out into the midst of the city, and he cried out with a loud and bitter cry.* ESV

Mordecai urged Esther to go the king and beg for mercy on behalf of her people. Esther ordered the Jews to fast for three days after which she would approach the king, even though it was against the law for the queen to do so without being invited. The king allowed her presence and asked why she had come to his court. She invited Haman and the king to a banquet at which she told them that if they would come to a second banquet on the following day she would inform them of her request.

What Do We Know?

Haman was so filled with hate and evil that when Mordecai would not bow down and pay homage to him, he was enraged. Somehow Haman contained himself! He went home and called his friends and wife to console him. He boasted about his position and told his wife and friends about his invitation to the second banquet. His wife and friends told him to build a gallows and ask the king to hang Mordecai in the morning. So by the time Haman went to the banquet in the afternoon the problem would have been dealt with and he could enjoy himself.

Haman was very pleased with the advice and he ordered a gallows to be built. He then proceeded to court to ask the king to hang Mordecai but was interrupted by the king's messengers. He was escorted to the king who asked him what should be done for someone the king wanted to honor. The king did not identify the honoree, but Haman assumed it to be himself. Haman told the king his recommendations for honoring a loyal servant and the king agreed, telling Haman to honor Mordecai just as Haman had described!

Devastated, Haman returned home and told Zeresh and their friends all that had happened. This time the group's advice was different:

> Esther 6:13b   *Then his wise men and his wife Zeresh said to him, "If Mordecai, before whom you have begun to fall, is of the Jewish people, you will not overcome him but will surely fall before him." ESV*

In Chapter 7 Haman was found out and the king hanged Haman on the very gallows he had built to hang Mordecai.

Implications and Observations

It is interesting to note that the book of Esther never mentions God! The reasons for this might be many – I will leave that for your thought and consideration (see A11).

The Jews were so moved by this story of Esther and Mordecai that an annual festival was instituted. It was called The Feast of Purim or The Feast of Lots, and celebrated the salvation of the Jews from the wicked Haman. Today the festival lasts two days and the custom is to light two candles, meet in the synagogue, have a short prayer and then read the book of Esther aloud.

Haman's plan was to annihilate the Jewish people. However, Haman took on an adversary he had no hope of overcoming – he just didn't realize that his adversary was God. God will not allow man's evil to destroy His plans for His chosen people.

Discussion Questions

A. GENERAL

A1. Why do you suppose Mordecai showed no fear of Haman? What is the historical background that might be the cause for this conflict between Haman and Mordecai?

A2. Wouldn't it have been easier for all concerned if Mordecai had been in step with secular customs and obeyed the decree when Haman passed by?

A3. Haman thought very highly of himself. What did he list as reasons he deserved to be thought of so highly?

A4. Did Haman have any valid reasons for boasting?

SECULAR:

SPIRITUAL:

Q. What does the Bible say a Christian should boast about?

A5. What triggered Haman's rant?

A6. Was Haman justified in taking some action?

Yes:

No:

A7. Why do you suppose God arranged that Haman would determine the honor that Mordecai would receive?

A8. Why did Esther invite Haman to the banquet? In your opinion, what might have been her motives?

A9. Esther 5:12-13   *Then Haman said, "Even Queen Esther let no one but me come with the king to the feast she prepared. And tomorrow also I am invited by her together with the king. 13 Yet all this is worth nothing to me, so long as I see Mordecai the Jew sitting at the king's gate."* ESV

Q. Did Haman do anything to earn the Queen's recognition or have anything to boast about?

Q. Do you see any irony between what Mordecai did and received and what Haman did and received?

A10. Contrast what happened in 6:4-6 with 3:8. What is the irony of this comparison?

Esther 3:8   *Then Haman said to King Ahasuerus, "There is a certain people scattered abroad and dispersed among the peoples in all the provinces of your kingdom. Their laws are different from those of every other people, and they do not keep the king's laws, so that it is not to the king's profit to tolerate them."* ESV

A11. What might be the reasons that God is not mentioned in this book? Do you think it is an accident or intentional? Why?

A12. God seems to be present in the story. List the evidence of God's sovereignty in the story.

A13. Why did Haman choose the honors listed in 6:8-9?

B. ZERESH'S ADVICE

B1. On what basis did Zeresh and Haman's friends give him advice? What was the basis of the relationship between Haman and his advisors?

B2. Why do you think they gave him this advice?

B3. Do you think Zeresh should have been included in the advising group? Why? Why not?

B4. Do you see any difference between Zeresh and the rest of the advising group?

B5. In general, why might it be important for Haman to have opinions from both friends and his wife?

B6. If you were part of the advising group of friends, what would you have asked Haman after he told you his story? If you were going to give him valuable advice, what specifically would you want to know before you offered your advice?

B7. Why did Haman like the advice of his wife and friends?

B8. List three characteristics you would look for in someone who was going to give you important advice.

D. APPLICATION

D1. Other than a spouse, do you have someone you trust to give you good advice?

D2. Are you undertaking or waging any battles you can't win?

D3. Have you ever gotten an inflated ego because of an award or honor you received? How did that work out?

D4. In 4:14 Mordecai made a statement to Esther that is timeless: "You may have been created for a time such as this."

> Esther 4:14   *If you keep silent at this time, liberation and deliverance will come to the Jewish people from another place, but you and your father's house will be destroyed. Who knows, perhaps you have come to the kingdom for such a time as this."*
>
> Q. For what were you created? Have you ever had a moment like this? Are you sure?

Blind Man
healed by Jesus

Occurrences of "blind man" in John 9: 2

Themes: Sin; Physical and Spiritual Blindness

NOTE: For simplicity we will refer to the blind man as the "blind man" both before and after he is healed.

Scripture

John 9 is not printed here as in the other lessons because in this study the chapter is outlined in the section titled, "*What Do We Know.*"

The Context

The Gospel of John describes only eight miracles of Jesus, called *signs*. This is the sixth sign. Prior to this healing sign John has reported, beginning in 8:31, conversations that Jesus was having about Abraham. Jesus said he knew the Jews were Abraham's descendants but that they were acting like the devil was their father, not Abraham. Jesus further stated that if they were truly Abraham's children, they would act like Abraham.

But Jesus continued to berate the people and said they belonged to their father, the devil, and they were not children of God. In 8:47

Jesus said that if they were children of God then they would hear what God said, but because they did not hear, then they were not His children.

The people respond by name-calling by calling: they called him a Samaritan and said he was demon-possessed. Jesus said their words were nonsense and then said that anyone who obeyed Him would never see death. This last statement caused further consternation and they asked Him if He was greater than Abraham. Jesus aggravated the Jews more when He said that He knew God, the Father, but they did not.

The Jews were still blinded to the truth and finally Jesus said He would tell them the truth: "before Abraham was, I am." (NIV) In effect, Jesus was claiming to be God. As a result of that statement the Jews prepared to stone Him (John 8:59), but Jesus slipped away. As He was walking along He came across a blind man.

What Do We Know?

John tells about several people and conversations in chapter 9. Although they all revolve around the healing of the blind man, they touch on other but related subjects. In order to better understand the different issues, I have outlined the story of the healing and its consequences under each character or group of characters in the story.

Disciples

- The disciples assumed that the man's blindness was due to either his sin or his parent's sin.

- Jesus stated that neither the blind man nor the parents had sinned.

Friends and Neighbors

- The neighbors wanted to know how his eyes were opened.

- They brought the blind man to the Pharisees, presumably to celebrate the healing and inform the Jewish leaders that a miracle had occurred.

Jesus

- Jesus told the disciples that the blindness was not due to sin.

- Jesus said the blindness occurred so God's work could be displayed in the blind man's life.

- Jesus healed the blind man. He mixed mud with saliva, put it on the blind man's eyes, and told him to wash it off in the Pool of Siloam.

- Jesus found the blind man after he'd been expelled by the Jews.

- Jesus asked if the blind man believed in the Son of Man.

- Jesus told the blind man that He was the Son of Man.

- The blind man believed and worshipped Jesus.

Blind Man (from blrth)

- He followed Jesus' instructions, washed off the mud, and came home with vision.

- He told his friends that Jesus healed him and described the process.

- His friends took him to the Pharisees, told them about Jesus, and claimed Jesus was a prophet.

- After talking with the parents, the Pharisees summoned the blind man and said Jesus was a sinner.

- The blind man said he knew nothing about Jesus being a sinner, but simply said, "I was blind and now I see."

- The Jews wanted to know how the blind man was healed.

- The blind man said, "I already told you. Why do you want to hear it again?"

- In response to the Pharisee's repeated demand for an explanation, the blind man asked them, "Do you want to become His disciples too?"

- The Jews got angry and said they didn't know anything about this Jesus.

- The blind man responded that it was remarkable they didn't know about Jesus, since Jesus performed a miracle and God doesn't do miracles through sinners.

- Finally, the blind man said that no one had ever done such a miracle before and if Jesus were not from God, He could do nothing, implying He must be from God.

- The Jews threw the blind man out (probably excommunicated him).

Pharisees/Jews
- The Pharisees asked the blind man how he was healed, and he repeated the story he had told his neighbors.

- John included the details that Jesus made the mud and healed the man on the Sabbath.

- Some Pharisees said Jesus could not be from God because He did not keep the Sabbath.

- Other Pharisees asked how a sinner could do miraculous signs.

- The Pharisees again asked the blind man about Jesus because they still did not believe the story.

- The Pharisees sent for the blind man's parents.

- They asked the parents how it was possible their son could now see, if he was really born blind.

- Getting nowhere with the parents, they summoned the blind man again.

- They threatened the blind man and said they knew that Jesus was a sinner (He worked on the Sabbath).

- When the blind man confirmed again that he could see, they asked him how Jesus opened his eyes.

- The blind man asked the Jews why they wanted to hear again: was it because they wanted to be His disciples too?

- The Jews became very angry and began insulting the blind man.

- The Jews accused the blind man of being Jesus' disciple, and claimed they were disciples of Moses.

- The blind man asked how they knew about Moses, but they didn't know about Jesus.

- The Jews responded to the blind man's claim that Jesus must be from God because no one had ever done such a miracle, by claiming he was steeped in sin since birth.

- The Jews became so angry, they threw the blind man out (probably refers to some form of excommunication).

Parents of the Blind Man

- The parents verified he was their son and was born blind.

- They didn't know how he regained his sight.

- They told the Pharisees to ask their son as "he can speak for himself."

- The parents were afraid of being thrown out of the synagogue if they claimed Jesus was the Messiah.

Implications and Observations

This chapter begins with Jesus and the disciples discussing sin. The disciples' assumption that either the blind man or his parents had sinned was the result of the prevailing thought that suffering was the result of sin. Good things happened to good people and bad things happened to bad people, even to the point that children could "inherit" the sins of their parents.

When the Pharisees tried to determine how the blind man was healed, some of them believed Jesus was a sinner because mixing the mud and putting it on the blind man's eyes constituted working on the Sabbath. The debate and doubt among the Pharisees about the healing revolved around the question of a sinner's ability to perform miraculous signs. The Pharisees were ready to believe that there was no miraculous healing even though the blind man could now see. The dilemma for the Pharisees was that the only alternative was that Jesus had in fact performed the miracle and therefore was sent from God. This dilemma is very similar to the Creationist and Evolutionist debate. The evolutionist will take his theories to the grave because the only viable alternative is the existence of a Creator God.

John 9 closes with the same subject on which it began: sin. This time, however, it is the sin of the Pharisees rather than that of the blind man. The Pharisees were blind to the truth of the Scriptures. Jesus said that if they were truly blind they would not be guilty of sin, but they claimed not to be blind. That is, they claimed to know the truth, but in fact they rejected it. They were, therefore, guilty.

The Pharisees were committed to their erroneous theological positions even though truth was all around them. Jesus, the Messiah, the Son of Man, the Son of God, and the Lord, was walking among them, just as the Scriptures had predicted, but they were spiritually blind. So the Pharisees tried to prove the blind man was not really blind, rather than trying to understand the meaning and implications of the miracle.

Being experts in the Scriptures, the Pharisees and scribes should have known that giving sight to the blind was prophesied by Isaiah as an expected activity of the coming Messiah:

> Isaiah 29:18   . . . *and out of their gloom and darkness the eyes of the blind shall see.* ESV

> Isaiah 35:5   *Then the eyes of the blind shall be opened, . . .* ESV

Discussion Questions

A. GENERAL

In John 9:2, the disciples asked Jesus who sinned because of a widespread belief in the "Retribution Principle." That principle said that good things happened to good people and bad things happened to bad people. Some believed that even the sin of the parents was passed to their children.

Job's three friends took the principle a step further, saying that if something bad happened to you, then you were sinful and must repent.

Q. How or why would this belief system about sin develop?

A2. Explain Jesus' response in John 9:3, "*Jesus answered, "It was not that this man sinned, or his parents, but that the works of God might be displayed in him." ESV*

Q. Does this say God caused the blindness?

A3. In 9:17 why would the Pharisees turn again for an explanation from the blind man?
John 9:17   *So they said again to the blind man, "What do you say about him, since he has opened your eyes?" He said, "He is a prophet." ESV*

A4. In 9:18, why do you think the Pharisees sent for the parents?
John 9:18   *The Jews did not believe that he had been blind and had received his sight, until they called the parents of the man who had received his sight.* ESV

A5. What did the parents tell the Pharisees and why? (See 9:21)

A6. In 9:24 the Pharisees told the blind man to "Give glory to God." What does that mean and why would they say that? (A similar instruction was given to Achan by Joshua in Joshua 7:19.)

A7. What was the result of the blind man's question? (Jn 9:27)
John 9:27   *He answered them, "I have told you already, and you would not listen. Why do you want to hear it again? Do you also want to become his disciples?"* ESV

Q. Do you think the blind man had the right to boldly challenge them or did he cross the line in 9:27?

A8. How would you characterize the exchanges between the blind man and the Pharisees in 9:26-34?

A9. What did the Pharisees mean when they said the blind man was Jesus' disciple? (9:28)

John 9:*28   And they reviled him, saying, "You are his disciple, but we are disciples of Moses." ESV*

A10. How did the Pharisees answer the blind man's explanation in 9:34?

Jn 9:34   *They answered him, "You were born in utter sin, and would you teach us?" And they cast him out. ESV*

B. HEALING ON THE SABBATH

B1. Why do you think Jesus used mud and saliva in this healing? Couldn't He just as easily have healed the blind man on the spot?

B2. John 9:14 indicates that the healing of the blind man took place on the Sabbath. Jesus also healed a sick man on the Sabbath at the pool of Bethesda (5:8-9). The Bethesda healing was the beginning of the conflict between Jesus and His enemies. What is the problem with healing on the Sabbath?

B3. Identify and explain the two positions in 9:16.

John 9:16   *Therefore some of the Pharisees said, "This man is not from God, for He doesn't keep the Sabbath!" But others were saying, "How can a sinful man perform such signs?" And there was a division among them.*

Q. What is wrong with these arguments?

C. OBSERVATIONS

C1. How did the blind man's understanding of Jesus change during the timeframe of chapter 9? Record how the blind man referred to or felt about Jesus in each of the following verses:

9:11 _____.
9:17 _____.
9:27 _____.
    (implying a teacher or prophet)
9:33 _____.
9:38 _____.

Q. This is a significant change. In a very short time the blind man's perception of Jesus went from seeing Him as a mere man to calling on Him as Lord. How would you explain this change of understanding?

Q. Compare this to how your understanding of Jesus has advanced since you first heard of Him.

C2. What was the blind man's assertion in 9:31?
John 9:31   *We know that God doesn't listen to sinners, but if anyone is God-fearing and does His will, He listens to him.*

Q. What do you think it means that God doesn't listen to sinners?

C3. We know that in general the blind man was correct. The Bible says that God does not "listen" to sinners, meaning He would not respond or answer prayers. This is confirmed in other passages:

> Ps 66:17-18   *I cried to him with my mouth, and high praise was on my tongue. 18 If I had cherished iniquity in my heart, the Lord would not have listened.* ESV

> Prov 28:9   *If one turns away his ear from hearing the law, even his prayer is an abomination.* ESV

> 1 Peter 3:7   *Likewise, husbands, live with your wives in an understanding way, showing honor to the woman as the weaker vessel, since they are heirs with you of the grace of life, so that your prayers may not be hindered.* ESV

> James 4:3   *You ask and do not receive, because you ask wrongly, to spend it on your passions.* ESV

> Q. How do we know this is a general truth and not an absolute truth?

C4. In 9:34 it says that they "threw him out." What do you think this means?

D. SPIRITUAL BLINDNESS

John 9:39-41   *Jesus said, "For judgment I came into this world, that those who do not see may see, and those who see may become blind." 40 Some of the Pharisees near him heard these things, and said to him, "Are we also blind?" 41 Jesus said to them, "If you were blind, you would have no guilt; but now that you say, 'We see,' your guilt remains."* ESV

D1. Explain in your own words the meaning of 9:41.

D2. What word or phrase would you use to describe the Pharisees and Jews in this story?

Q. What do you think caused this situation with the Pharisees?

E. APPLICATION

E1. Are you blind about some spiritual things? Have you established a position about God, Jesus, the Holy Spirit, or Scripture that is impacting your relationship with God?

> a. Is there anything in the Bible that you don't believe or don't understand?

> b. Is there anything your church claims as truth that you don't believe or don't understand?

E2. Has the work of God been displayed in any way in your life? Have you ever suffered or been blessed such that others might see and praise God?

E3. Has anyone ever challenged your faith to the point you had to defend yourself? How did you do?

E4. Is arrogance, pride, ego, or self-righteousness impacting your faith or relationships in any way?

E5. Do you know anyone who is blind to spiritual things? How could you help them?

Shadrach-Meshack-Abednego
(Hananiah-Mishael-Azariah)
Daniel's friends

Occurrences of "Shadrach . . ." in Book of Daniel: 15
Occurrences of "Hananiah . . ." in Book of Daniel: 5

Themes: Trust in God; Compromise

NOTE: All three men are always mentioned together; they are never mentioned separately.

Scripture

Daniel 3

King Nebuchadnezzar made an image of gold, whose height was sixty cubits and its breadth six cubits. He set it up on the plain of Dura, in the province of Babylon. 2 Then King Nebuchadnezzar sent to gather the satraps, the prefects, and the governors, the counselors, the treasurers, the justices, the magistrates, and all the officials of the provinces to come to the dedication of the image that King Nebuchadnezzar had set up. 3 Then the satraps, the prefects, and the governors, the counselors, the treasurers, the justices, the magistrates, and all the officials of the provinces gathered for the dedication of the image that King Nebuchadnezzar had set up. And they stood before the image that Nebuchadnezzar had set up. 4 And the herald proclaimed aloud, "You are commanded, O peoples, nations, and languages, 5 that when you hear the sound of the horn, pipe, lyre, trigon, harp, bagpipe, and every kind of music, you are to fall down and worship the golden image that King Nebuchadnezzar has set up. 6 And whoever does

43

not fall down and worship shall immediately be cast into a burning fiery furnace." 7 Therefore, as soon as all the peoples heard the sound of the horn, pipe, lyre, trigon, harp, bagpipe, and every kind of music, all the peoples, nations, and languages fell down and worshiped the golden image that King Nebuchadnezzar had set up.

The Fiery Furnace

8 Therefore at that time certain Chaldeans came forward and maliciously accused the Jews. 9 They declared to King Nebuchadnezzar, "O King, live forever! 10 You, O King, have made a decree, that every man who hears the sound of the horn, pipe, lyre, trigon, harp, bagpipe, and every kind of music, shall fall down and worship the golden image. 11 And whoever does not fall down and worship shall be cast into a burning fiery furnace. 12 There are certain Jews whom you have appointed over the affairs of the province of Babylon: Shadrach, Meshach, and Abednego. These men, O King, pay no attention to you; they do not serve your gods or worship the golden image that you have set up."

13 Then Nebuchadnezzar in furious rage commanded that Shadrach, Meshach, and Abednego be brought. So they brought these men before the King. 14 Nebuchadnezzar answered and said to them, "Is it true, O Shadrach, Meshach, and Abednego, that you do not serve my gods or worship the golden image that I have set up? 15 Now if you are ready when you hear the sound of the horn, pipe, lyre, trigon, harp, bagpipe, and every kind of music, to fall down and worship the image that I have made, well and good. But if you do not worship, you shall immediately be cast into a burning fiery furnace. And who is the god who will deliver you out of my hands?"

16 Shadrach, Meshach, and Abednego answered and said to the King, "O Nebuchadnezzar, we have no need to answer you in this matter. 17 If this be so, our God whom we serve is able to deliver us from the burning fiery furnace, and he will deliver us out of your hand, O King. 18 But if not, be it known to you, O King, that we will not serve your gods or worship the golden image that you have set up."

19 Then Nebuchadnezzar was filled with fury, and the expression of his face was changed against Shadrach, Meshach, and Abednego. He ordered the furnace heated seven times more than it was usually heated. 20 And he ordered some of the mighty men of his army to bind Shadrach, Meshach, and Abednego, and to cast them into the burning fiery furnace. 21 Then these men were bound in their cloaks, their tunics, their hats, and their other garments, and they were thrown into the burning fiery furnace. 22 Because the King's order was urgent and the furnace overheated, the flame of the fire killed those men who took up Shadrach, Meshach, and Abednego. 23 And these three men, Shadrach, Meshach, and Abednego, fell bound into the burning fiery furnace.

24 Then King Nebuchadnezzar was astonished and rose up in haste. He declared to his counselors, "Did we not cast three men bound into the fire?" They answered and said to the King, "True, O King." 25 He answered and said, "But I see four men unbound, walking in the midst of the fire, and they are not hurt; and the appearance of the fourth is like a son of the gods."

26 Then Nebuchadnezzar came near to the door of the burning fiery furnace; he declared, "Shadrach, Meshach, and Abednego, servants of the Most High God, come out, and come here!" Then Shadrach, Meshach, and Abednego came out from the fire. 27 And the satraps, the prefects, the governors, and the King's counselors gathered together and saw that the fire had not had any power over the bodies of those men. The hair of their heads was not singed, their cloaks were not harmed, and no smell of fire had come upon them. 28 Nebuchadnezzar answered and said, "Blessed be the God of Shadrach, Meshach, and Abednego, who has sent his angel and delivered his servants, who trusted in him, and set aside the King's command, and yielded up their bodies rather than serve and worship any god except their own God. 29 Therefore I make a decree: Any people, nation, or language that speaks anything against the God of Shadrach, Meshach, and Abednego shall be torn limb from limb, and their houses laid in ruins, for there is no other god who is able to rescue in this way." 30 Then the King promoted Shadrach, Meshach, and Abednego in the province of Babylon. ESV

Context

Daniel and his Jewish friends were in captivity in Babylon at the time of Nebuchadnezzar. In Chapter 1 the King decreed that the young men should eat royal food but Daniel and his friends refused the King's food and asked for a special diet. They thrived on this special diet and God blessed the four young men with knowledge and understanding. In Chapter 2 the King had a dream and God interpreted that dream through Daniel resulting in the King falling down in homage to Daniel. The King placed Daniel "in a high position" in his royal court and also appointed Shadrach, Meshach, and Abednego to manage the province of Babylon.

In Chapter 3 the King dedicated a gold statue of himself. He declared that all people were to fall down and worship the statue, but Shadrach, Meshach, and Abednego refused to obey the King's order.

What Do We Know?

What does it require on our part to trust God? Probably the best encouragement is actually to experience the positive results of trusting Him. The Bible has a great deal to say about what is necessary on our part to experience the love of God that comes from trusting in Him.

Psalm 78:7 tells us that the laws and statues of God should be passed down to our children and when that happens, "*Then they would put their trust in God and would not forget his deeds but would keep his commands.*" Dt 28:9 tells us that He will establish us if we obey His commands and walk in His ways. If we desire God's favor, there is certainly the expectation that we are living a life of obedience to His ways.

This is confirmed again in Psalm 37:5 which says to commit our ways to Him. If we pledge ourselves to follow His ways then He will act on our behalf. Ps 37:6 goes on to say that in acting on our behalf He will make our righteousness shine like the sun at dawn. Psalm 37:1-11 provides us with wisdom in regard to our relationship with God. A series of instructions describes the ideal nature of our relationship with Him:

37:3   Trust in the Lord and do good
37:4   Delight in the Lord
37:5   Commit your way to the Lord
37:7   Be still before the Lord; wait patiently for Him
37:9   Hope in the Lord
37:11   The meek will inherit the land

Additionally Psalm 37:34 and 40 say:
37:34   Wait for the Lord
37:40   Take refuge in Him

These instructions give us a clear view of what our Lord desires in regard to our relationship with Him. And Ps 62:8 tells us further to trust in the Lord at <u>all</u> times. Regardless of our circumstances we should pour out our hearts to Him, Seek refuge in Him and trust in Him at all times.

> *May the God of hope fill you with all joy and peace*
> *as you <u>trust</u> in him, so that you may overflow*
> *with hope by the power of the Holy Spirit.*
> (Ro 15:13 NIV)

Implications and Observations

A faithful Jesus-follower trusts in and depends on God in both good times and bad. When I put my trust in God and the truth of Scripture, the challenges in my worldly life do not shake my trust in God and His promises. Trusting God on a daily basis is possible only if (1) we know His character, and (2) we know His Word. We will trust Him because we know that He is faithful and that He always keeps His promises. Based on that trust, we develop confidence in His oversight of our lives.

Faith and trust are not generated on their own! Trust is only possible as we know God, know His Word, and become convinced of His faithfulness. Worry, fear, and distrust are the result of focusing on our circumstances instead of claiming and *depending on God's promises*. As we grow in the knowledge of Him and His Word, we grow in spiritual understanding and develop trust so that we know we can depend on Him even when life gets difficult.

Challenge Question

How much cash would it take for you to seriously violate your moral or religious standards?

$1000 - $2 million - $5 million - $15 million - $25 million - $50 million?

For example: robbery, murder, adultery, leaving or rejecting the church, abandoning your family, blaspheming Jesus, etc.

Q. In thinking how someone might respond to the temptation to sin, how would you order the following in your thinking process?

1) Do I want to do it or not?
2) What will I gain and what do I risk?
3) Is it good/legal or evil/illegal?
4) Will others know or not know I did it?
5) How long will I or must I do this?
6) How will it impact my friends or family?
7) Is it right or wrong as judged by the world's values?
8) Is it good or evil as judged by God?

Q. Which question would *most people* put at the top of the list?

Discussion Questions

A. DANIEL CHAPTER 3

A1. Why do you think the King erected the large gold image?

Q. What was the image?

A2. Exactly what were the people told to do, and who told the King that the three were rebelling against the order?

A3. Given the three refused to bow down and worship the King's image, how would you describe their spiritual character?

A4. What do you see as the overall characteristic of their faith?

Q. Do you think the three believed that God would save them?

A5. How would you describe the King's response to this miracle?

A6. What test did the King propose? (3:15)

Q. What was the purpose of this challenge?

A7. What does it mean when the three said they did not need to answer for God (3:16)? Note that 3:16 says they didn't need to give an answer to the question in 3:15 which was, "Who is the god that can rescuc you from my power?"

A8. How would you describe the reply of the three men in 3:17-18? What did the three believe?

A9. Who was the fourth person in the fire?

A10. Who did the King say the person looks like?

A11. What does the text say the King believed after the three came out of the fire?

A12. Do you think the King was a "believer"?

B. TRUST

B1. The Bible gives some great examples of men who trusted God:

Gen 6:5-22 - In faith Noah built an ark.
Gen 22: 1-12 - Abraham was willing to sacrifice Isaac.

1 Sam 17:45-47 - David challenged and killed Goliath.

Daniel 6:23 - Daniel entered the lion's den.

Q. What are some common themes in these examples?

Q. Do you know anyone with this type of faith/trust? What drives then?

B2. How would you define trust in God?

B3. How does one develop and cultivate the ability to trust? Why can one person trust and another cannot?

B4. God's word does not say that when we say we trust Him, He showers us with all kinds of benefits. What are the requirements in the two passages below in order for God to respond to our dependence on Him?

1) Ps 9:10   *And those who know your name put their trust in you, for you, O Lord, have not forsaken those who seek you.* ESV

PROMISE: _____.

REQUIREMENTS: _____.

2) Psalm 37:5-6   *Commit your way to the Lord; trust in him, and he will act. 6 He will bring forth your righteousness as the light, and your justice as the noonday.* ESV

PROMISE: _____.

REQUIREMENTS:_____.

C. COMPROMISE

C1. *I'll compromise just this one time.*
What if the three young men had agreed that they would worship the idol just one time and then avoid doing so in the future?

C2. *I'll just play along and it won't mean anything to me.*
What if the three young men had thought they would avoid trouble by just playing along with the King, and that God would know that in their hearts they didn't really worship the gold image?

C3. *It's the law, I don't have any choice.*
What if the three men had said to themselves that it was a decree of the King or a law of the land and they were obligated to obey?

C4. *We must do anything to stay alive.*
What if the three young men had thought that they must do whatever was necessary to stay alive and continue to serve the Lord because by dying they could not be any use to God?

C5. *God will forgive us.*
What if the three young men thought that their sin would be forgiven, especially under these circumstances?

D. APPLICATION

D1. Do life's trials, temptations, difficulties or actual suffering impact your faith and trust in God? Why? Why not?

D2. Do you have any reason to take a stand for something or someone today like Shadrach, Meshach, and Abednego?

> Q. If you took a stand, who in your circle of family or friends would support you? Should you talk with them first?

D3. What are the hindrances in your life that fight against trusting God?

> Q. What would make those hindrances go away?

D4. What will you do if you have an "opportunity" to take the mark of the beast, or any other serious temptation in life?

Aeneas
the paralyzed man in Lydda

Occurrences of "Aeneas" in the Bible: 2

Theme: Jesus heals

Scripture

Acts 9:31-35   *So the church throughout all Judea and Galilee and Samaria had peace and was being built up. And walking in the fear of the Lord and in the comfort of the Holy Spirit, it multiplied.*

The Healing of Aeneas
32 Now as Peter went here and there among them all, he came down also to the saints who lived at Lydda. 33 There he found a man named Aeneas, bedridden for eight years, who was paralyzed. 34 And Peter said to him, "Aeneas, Jesus Christ heals you; rise and make your bed." And immediately he rose. 35 And all the residents of Lydda and Sharon saw him, and they turned to the Lord. ESV

The Context:

The first thing the text tells us is that the church was at peace. The three geographic areas mentioned encompassed most of what we would consider Israel. Jerusalem was in Judea, and both Samaria and Galilee were north of Judea. Lydda was about 25 miles northwest of Jerusalem and 12 miles from Joppa on the coast. The church had previously been driven out of Jerusalem:

> Acts 8:1 *And Saul approved of his* [Stephen's] *execution. And there arose on that day a great persecution against the church in Jerusalem, and they were all scattered throughout the regions of Judea and Samaria, except the apostles.* ESV

But at this time there was peace and the church was growing again. Saul (Paul) had been converted on the road to Damascus and was no longer carrying out murderous deeds against the church. These three geographic locations probably represent much of the church at that time. Stephen's death occurred around 35 AD (Acts 7:57-60). Since this was very soon after Pentecost, there would have been relatively few believers outside Israel.

Other than the fact of its existence, we know little about the church in Lydda. Peter arrived in Lydda and healed a man who had been paralyzed for eight years. We know from earlier chapters in Acts that this was not the first healing or miracle performed by Peter or one of the other Apostles before coming to Lydda:

Healings

- Lame man at the Beautiful Gate (3:1-10).
- Sick carried out into streets for healing (5:15).
- Large group of sick from surrounding towns, as well as those tormented by unclean spirits (5:16).
- The demon-possessed, paralyzed, and lame (8:7).

Miracles, Wonders, and Signs

- The Apostles performed many wonders and signs (2:43).
- The Apostles performed many signs and wonders among the people (5:12).
- Stephen performed great wonders and signs among the people (6:8).
- Philip performed signs (8:6).
- Philip performed signs and great miracles (8:13).

What Do We Know?

When Peter met Aeneas, the paralyzed man, he told the man that Jesus Christ healed him. Immediately Aeneas got up. The text says nothing about Aeneas, his faith, whether he asked to be healed, or what he did after the healing. Luke, the author, simply reports that he got up immediately.

The result of this miracle was that all who lived in the area of Lydda and Sharon saw the healed man and turned to the Lord. "Sharon" may refer to the Plain of Sharon, which is west and northwest of Lydda. This Plain was bounded on the west by the Mediterranean Sea and on the east by the foothills of Samaria (Mt. Ephraim and the Carmel range). On the other hand, Sharon may refer to a small village close to Lydda. The geographic location is not significant in this story.

This account, although short, provides several key bits of information:

- There was a church in Lydda. We are not told whether or not Aeneas was a part of that church.
- Aeneas had been paralyzed and bedridden for 8 years.

- Peter pronounced his healing by Jesus.
- Peter told Aeneas to get up and he immediately got up.
- Peter told him to pick up his bed (mat).
- All the people saw him so it is probable that he went around town telling them about the miracle.

Just as in the case of Shamgar (the judge who killed 600 Philistines), there is a great deal more that we do not know:

- We don't know whether or not Aeneas was a believer. Nothing was said about his faith.
- We don't know if Peter went looking specifically for Aeneas or if he just happened upon him while visiting the church.
- We do not know why Aeneas was paralyzed or how old he was. The text tells us he was a man, so we know he was an adult. It also says he had been paralyzed and bedridden for eight years, so he was probably not handicapped from birth.
- We do not know if Peter touched Aeneas physically or just pronounced him healed.
- We don't know where this took place.
- We do not know if he picked up his bed (mat) or not.
- We do not know if anyone besides Peter was present at the time of the healing.
- We do not know the size of the church or the population in Lydda and Sharon. Since "all" the people turned to the Lord, it would be reasonable to assume that the population was small.
- We do not know if the people turned to the Lord because of Aeneas' healing and testimony or because the church in Lydda effectively shared the Gospel.
- We do not know what impact, if any, this healing miracle had on the spread of the church beyond Lydda.

Implications and Observations

It is reasonable to assume that the healing miracle, and not the preaching, teaching, or evangelism was the catalyst for people turning to the Lord. It is probably fair to assume that Aeneas was a well-known individual in the community and his friends and neighbors would have been overjoyed at his healing. The first question everyone would naturally ask would be how the healing occurred. So Peter, Aeneas, and the church would have had an easy transition to a spiritual conversation.

We can probably conclude that this healing would have been an overwhelming surprise to Aeneas. There is no indication that he had requested any of the Apostles to heal him. Aeneas' life changed dramatically because of this miracle. In one minute he was able to walk! Before the healing, Aeneas' life was restricted to a bed in one room and afterward he could go anywhere he wanted and live a normal life.

If it is literally true that ALL in the community were saved, this would have been a unique community. Everyone would have been walking with God and the dynamic of the town would have been very different than it had been in the past.

Discussion Questions

A GENERAL

A1. This isolated healing seems unnecessary for the overall narrative because in the next passage we read the report of Peter raising Tabitha (Dorcas) to life after she died. Why do you think this story is reported here?

A2. How would you guess the success of this healing impacted Peter? Do you think it would have influenced him in any way with Dorcas? (9:36ff)

A3. Luke, the author of Acts, gives little detail concerning Aeneas' healing. What are the things that were not reported in this story that we often see in other Bible accounts about healings?

A4. How would you compare the healing of the man with leprosy (Lk 5:12-16) with the healing of Aeneas?

A5. What does it mean that the church "had peace"? (9:31)

A6. Why would "peace" have anything to do with the church growing?

A7. Do you think that the "peace" had anything to do with Paul being sent off to Tarsus (9:30)?

A8. Do you think this kind of healing, (1) could happen today, (2) does happen today, or (3) is not likely to happen at all?

A9. How would Aeneas' life change? Compare his life before and after his healing.

BEFORE:

AFTER:

Q. What would you assume Aeneas did after the healing?

Q. What would you have done?

A10. Compare life in the town before the healing to life in the town after everyone had turned to the Lord. How would the dynamics of the town, relationships, business dealings, etc., have changed after this event? How different would it have been?

BEFORE:

AFTER:

A11. Why did all the people turn to the Lord after the miracle?

A12. Hearing about and then seeing the result of a miracle would not necessarily cause someone to turn to the Lord. What else would have had to take place after the people saw Aeneas walking?

A13. What does it mean that the church was walking "in the encouragement of the Holy Spirit"?

A14. If you were Aeneas talking to a neighbor after the healing, what would you say?

A15. If you were a church member talking to an unbelieving neighbor after the healing, how would you explain the healing so that the unbeliever would turn to the Lord?

A16. Compare and consider the differences between Peter's healing of Aeneas and His healing of the paralytic in Luke 5:17-26.

Jesus healing of paralytic:	Peter healing Aeneas:
Friends carry paralytic to Jesus	_____.
Large crowds prevent access	_____.
Extraordinary measures to reach Jesus	_____.
Friends and paralytic demonstrate great faith	_____.
Jesus forgave paralytic's sin before healing	_____.
Jesus told paralytic to take mat and go home	_____.
Man immediately got up	_____.
Man went home praising God	_____.
Everyone else gave praise to God	_____.
All filled with awe (amazement)	_____.
Nothing said about anyone being saved	_____.

Q. What can you conclude from the above comparison?

A17. Are there life lessons here, or is this just a story about Peter healing a man?

C. FEAR OF THE LORD

C1. What does it mean that the church was walking in the "fear of the Lord"?

C2. How might this "fear" have contributed to the healing miracle?

D. APPLICATION

D1. Do you believe that Jesus heals? Why? Why not?

D2. Where do you need healing in your life? Is the power of Jesus required?

D3. Are you living in peace? If not, why not? What would be necessary to bring peace into your life?

D4. After your week of study, what one thing do you personally want to take away from this lesson?

Alexander
the coppersmith

Occurrences of "Alexander" in the Bible: 2

Themes: Blasphemy, False Teachers, Traitors

NOTE: For the purposes of this study we are going to assume that both scripture references below refer to the same Alexander. There are also two mentions of an Alexander in the Book of Acts but we will assume they do not refer to this Alexander, who was a coppersmith.

Scripture

<u>1 Tim 1:18-20</u>
This charge I entrust to you, Timothy, my child, in accordance with the prophecies previously made about you, that by them you may wage the good warfare, 19 holding faith and a good conscience. By rejecting this, some have made shipwreck of their faith, 20 among whom are Hymenaeus and Alexander, whom I have handed over to Satan that they may learn not to blaspheme. ESV

<u>2 Tim 4:14-15</u>
14 Alexander the coppersmith did me great harm; the Lord will repay him according to his deeds. 15 Beware of him yourself, for he strongly opposed our message. ESV

The Context

Much of Paul's New Testament writings are directed to the churches he founded on his four missionary journeys. One of those was in Ephesus, where Paul's protégé Timothy was located. Paul wrote to encourage him and to counsel him concerning some existing problems. The two men obviously had a very close relationship. Paul described Timothy as "my true child in the faith." This description may imply that Paul led Timothy to a saving relationship with Christ or simply that they were very good friends and co-workers.

In his first letter to Timothy Paul warned him about Alexander. Paul wrote to Timothy in Ephesus, instructing him about false teaching, worship, and appointing qualified leaders for the church. At the end of the first chapter, Paul warned him specifically about two men, Hymenaeus and Alexander, who had blasphemed. Paul made no further comment about Alexander in this first letter.

In Paul's second letter to Timothy, written two to four years later from prison (see 2 Tim 2:9), he again warned Timothy about issues and problems that would endanger the church. Paul even suggested that Timothy may have to suffer as he ministered to the church (2 Tim 2:3). In the last chapter of this letter, Paul repeated his warning about Alexander, and told Timothy to be on guard because Alexander strongly opposed the Gospel.

Discussion Questions

A. FIRST LETTER (1 Tim 1:18-20)

A1. Based on 1 Tim 1:19 what did Paul imply about the nature of Hymenaeus and Alexander's rebellion?

A2. The harm that Alexander did was probably related to his blasphemy. What is your personal understanding about what it means to blaspheme?

A3. Alexander is described as blaspheming. Do you remember anyone else in the Bible who was accused of blaspheming, other than Jesus? Who were they and what happened to them?

A4. How do we know that blasphemy is a serious offense?

A5. Why do <u>you</u> think Paul believed that handing Alexander over to Satan (excluding him from the church) would teach him anything?

A6. What do you think Paul meant when he said they will *"learn"* not to blaspheme?

A7. Do you think that Alexander would be more or less hostile if he were expelled from the church?

A8. Assuming that at one time Alexander was a follower, why would he act in this manner?

B. SECOND LETTER (2 Tim 4:14-15)

B1. What evidence is there that the Alexander referred to in 1 Tim 1:20 is the same Alexander as mentioned in 2 Tim 4:14?

B2. In 4:14 Paul said that Alexander did him a great deal of harm. What might Paul be talking about? What kind of harm? What kind of problems may have been created?

B3. Do you know anyone who caused great harm to the church? What happened?

B4. Who did Paul say would mete out punishment and what is the significance?

B5. What do you suspect Paul meant when he said that the Lord would repay Alexander for what he had done?

B6. What will be the basis of the punishment?

B7. Thus, what is the basis of the severity of the punishment?

C. APPLICATION

C1. Have you ever refused to believe or act rightly, even though your conscience told you to do something else? What happened? What were the consequences?

C2. Have you ever intentionally opposed the Gospel? What happened? If not, do you know anyone who did?

C3. What do you think should be done with a <u>church member</u> who is extremely disruptive and openly speaks against Jesus or Christian beliefs?

C4. Do you know anyone who has blasphemed or was accused of blasphemy? What happened? How did it impact you?

C5. What would you do if a friend or acquaintance in the church was, in your opinion, blaspheming or very near blaspheming?

C6. Do you think it is right to walk away from someone who simply refuses to listen?

Slave Girl
with spirit that predicts future

> **Occurrences of this "slave girl" in the Bible:** 1
> There are four pronoun references to this slave girl.
>
> **Themes:** Demon Possession; Healing; Persecution

Scripture

Acts 16:16-24

As we were going to the place of prayer, we were met by a slave girl who had a spirit of divination and brought her owners much gain by fortune-telling. 17 She followed Paul and us, crying out, "These men are servants of the Most High God, who proclaim to you the way of salvation." 18 And this she kept doing for many days. Paul, having become greatly annoyed, turned and said to the spirit, "I command you in the name of Jesus Christ to come out of her." And it came out that very hour.

19 But when her owners saw that their hope of gain was gone, they seized Paul and Silas and dragged them into the marketplace before the rulers. 20 And when they had brought them to the magistrates, they said, "These men are Jews, and they are disturbing our city. 21 They advocate customs that are not lawful for us as Romans to accept or practice." 22 The crowd joined in attacking them, and the magistrates tore the garments off them and gave orders to beat them with rods. 23 And when they had inflicted many blows upon them, they threw them into prison, ordering the jailer to keep them safely. 24 Having received this order, he put them into the inner prison and fastened their feet in the stocks. ESV

The Context

This story occurs in Acts immediately following the conversion of Lydia (dealer in purple cloth) and her household in or near Philippi. The passage in the NIV begins with "Once when we were going," therefore this occurrence does not necessarily relate to their visit in Philippi, but that would be a reasonable deduction.

At the end of this story Paul and Silas were thrown into jail. If we continue reading we find that at midnight the jail was shaken and the doors flew open. However, Paul and Silas did not leave the jail because they feared for the life of the jailer who would have been held responsible for their escape. This resulted in the jailer and all his family being baptized.

What Do We Know?

The nature of the slave girl's spirit is described differently in various translations:

Acts 16:16   slave girl who had a spirit of divination (ESV, NRSV)
Acts 16:16   slave girl possessed with a spirit of divination (NKJV)
Acts 16:16   slave girl ran into us. She was a psychic (The MESSAGE)

The Greek word for "spirit" in this verse refers to a "python spirit." This is generally considered a reference to a mythical snake which was worshipped in some pagan cultures. It clearly referred to a demonic spirit, not a good or benevolent one.

The NIV translation indicates that the slave girl "predicted the future." There is no other information given about this ability or even if the predictions were true. She is described as a "fortune-teller." One might compare her to self-proclaimed fortune-tellers today who weave enough vague truths into their predictions that naïve people overlook incorrect predictions and remember their truths or near truths.

Discussion Questions

A. GENERAL

A1. What does 16:17 tell us about who is traveling with Paul?

A2. List all you learn in 16:17 about the slave girl's spirit.

A3. What does this tell us about the "powers" of this demon?

A4. Why do you think the spirit referred to Paul and Silas as "slaves"?

A5. Why would the slave girl or spirit do this for days? What was to be gained?

A6. Why do you think Paul was greatly aggravated, given that the spirit was speaking truth, at least as far as we know?

A7. Why do you think Paul chose to exorcise the demon?

A8. Why do you think it was so easy to exorcise the demon?

A9. Do you think Paul and Silas were within their legal rights to exorcise the demon?

A10. What did the slave owners claim before the magistrates?

A11. Promoting various and different religions in the Roman Empire was not illegal, unless it led to civil unrest or active confrontation with authorities. So what were the "unlawful customs?"

A12. If Paul had been given a chance to respond to the charges, what do you think he would have said?

A13. What is inconsistent between 16:19 and 16:20-21?

A14. What customs do you think the slave owners were referring to when they said "illegal practices"?

A15. What caused the magistrates to act so rashly?

Q. Would this be normal for Roman magistrates?

A16. Do you think the magistrates did anything illegal?

A17. Why would the magistrates want Paul and Silas to be "securely guarded"?

B. APPLICATION

B1. Have you ever had an experience with a person you thought may have been demon possessed? How did you react? How should you have reacted?

B2. Have you ever abruptly reacted to some stimulus and then wished that you had considered your response first?

B3. Have you ever been charged falsely for something? How did you handle the situation? What did you learn?

B4. Do you know anyone who believes in fortune tellers or reading tarot cards?

B5. The slave girl is described as a fortune teller. Have you ever met a fortune teller? Have you ever had your fortune told at a fair or carnival just for the fun of it? What were your expectations?

Q. Did the "prophecies" of your fortuneteller come true?

Q. What did you think about the person doing the fortune telling? Did you trust him/her?

Q. Did you believe him/her? Why? Why not?

Crippled Man at Lystra
with faith

Occurrences of "crippled" in the Bible: 1

Themes: Healing Faith; Physical Healing;
Mistaken Worship; Persecution

Scripture

<u>Acts 14:8-20</u>   <u>Paul and Barnabas at Lystra</u>

*Now at Lystra there was a man sitting who could not use his feet.
He was crippled from birth and had never walked. 9 He listened to
Paul speaking. And Paul, looking intently at him and seeing that he
had faith to be made well, 10 said in a loud voice, "Stand upright on
your feet." And he sprang up and began walking. 11 And when the
crowds saw what Paul had done, they lifted up their voices, saying
in Lycaonian, "The gods have come down to us in the likeness of
men!" 12 Barnabas they called Zeus, and Paul, Hermes, because he
was the chief speaker. 13 And the priest of Zeus, whose temple was
at the entrance to the city, brought oxen and garlands to the gates
and wanted to offer sacrifice with the crowds. 14 But when the
apostles Barnabas and Paul heard of it, they tore their garments
and rushed out into the crowd, crying out, 15 "Men, why are you
doing these things? We also are men, of like nature with you, and*

we bring you good news, that you should turn from these vain things to a living God, who made the heaven and the earth and the sea and all that is in them. 16 In past generations he allowed all the nations to walk in their own ways. 17 Yet he did not leave himself without witness, for he did good by giving you rains from heaven and fruitful seasons, satisfying your hearts with food and gladness." 18 Even with these words they scarcely restrained the people from offering sacrifice to them.

Paul Stoned at Lystra

19 But Jews came from Antioch and Iconium, and having persuaded the crowds, they stoned Paul and dragged him out of the city, supposing that he was dead. 20 But when the disciples gathered about him, he rose up and entered the city, and on the next day he went on with Barnabas to Derbe. ESV

The Context

Prior to arriving in Lystra, Paul and Barnabas had been in Iconium where they had experienced both success and failure. After speaking at the synagogue a great number of both Jews and Gentile Greeks had believed. But the Jews who rejected the Gospel created a firestorm of protest. Paul and Barnabas stayed on in Iconium to confront the agitators and even performed signs and wonders.

However, the people were divided. The troublemakers decided to stone Paul and Barnabas but the believers uncovered the plan and fled to Lystra where they healed a crippled man. It is instructive to observe that Paul's rejection in Iconium did not cause him to abandon his mission. He simply fled from those who were trying to harm him, went into the countryside, and continued to preach.

Upon arrival in Lystra Paul and Barnabas observed a crippled man who was lame from birth – he had never walked. The text intentionally points out that the crippled man listened to Paul as he spoke.

Discussion Questions:

A. GENERAL:

A1. Why did Paul heal the crippled man?

A2. Why do you think the text says that Paul observed the crippled man *closely*?

A3. Do you see any significance in the text "*he had faith to be made well*"?

A4. Do you think this is the same distinction as "belief" and "saving faith"?

A5. How did Paul know he had faith to be healed? What did Paul see?

A6. Since it is never reported that one of the disciples tried to perform a healing and it did not occur, what would you conclude about the disciples' ability to heal?

A7. What is amazing about 14:10?

A8. What did the people witnessing the healing say upon seeing the miracle? Why?

A9. The people credited the healing to the Greek gods, Zeus and Hermes. Do you find this surprising?

A10. Is the reaction about the identity of Paul and Barnabas as Greek gods surprising?

A11. A Greek priest from a Greek temple outside the city arrived. What did he do?

A12. Where did the priest get the bulls and wreaths?

A13. What is amazing about the last part of 14:13?

A14. What did Paul and Barnabas do (not what they said)? What is the meaning?

A15. List specifically the different points of what Paul and the disciples shouted to the crowd:

a. _____.

b. _____.

c. _____.

d. _____.

e. _____.

f. However, you should have recognized His existence because He has shown kindness:

by giving _____.

by providing _____ _____.

and by filling _____.

A16. How did Paul and Silas describe the Greek gods?

A17. How did the people respond (14:18)?

A18. Then Jews from outside Lystra (from Antioch and Iconium) came and turned the crowd against Paul and Barnabas. How could outside Jews turn the people against Paul and Barnabas so quickly?

A19. Why would the local people want to stone Paul?

A20. Do you think that Paul was dead or unconscious when they dragged him out of the city after stoning him?

A21. If Paul was dead or nearly dead what caused him to "get up"?

A22. Based on Mt 14:21-23 what do we know about the church in Lystra?

B. HEALING PRAYER (JAMES 5:13-15)

Is anyone among you suffering? Let him pray. Is anyone cheerful? Let him sing praise. 14 Is anyone among you sick? Let him call for the elders of the church, and let them pray over him, anointing him with oil in the name of the Lord. 15 And the prayer of faith will save the one who is sick, and the Lord will raise him up. And if he has committed sins, he will be forgiven. ESV

The reference to oil in this passage could have several possible meanings:

- Oil (olive oil) was used medicinally and the reference might refer to using oil to help heal.
- It could also be used to heighten the importance and sacredness, both mentally and emotionally, of the serious nature of the prayer that is being offered for healing.
- It might be used as a symbol of the Holy Spirit representing the power of God.

- It may serve as an aid to faith.
- Regardless of the use or non-use of oil, the power is in the prayer and God's sovereign response.

B1. How is healing prayer described or defined in James 5:13-15?

B2. What is a "prayer of faith"?

B3. Have you ever prayed and received an immediate answer to your prayer? If so, why do you think that happened?

C. APPLICATION

C1. Have you ever been thought of as something or someone more than you are? What happened? Did it end well or badly?

C2. Have you ever worshipped false gods? Or have you ever allowed someone or something to be more important than Jesus? What happened?

C3. If you make gods of preachers (pastors), your worship is misplaced. Have you or do you know people who put their pastors on pedestals? What is the danger in these situations?

Transformation Road Map

Primary Takeaways

1: Rebellion against God-appointed authority, driven by dissatisfaction and pride, leads to severe consequences and lasting damage that cannot be fully undone.

2: God's providence works behind the scenes to protect His people and thwart the plans of those who oppose them, even when His presence is not explicitly mentioned.

3: The healing of the blind man in John 9 reveals that spiritual blindness is a deliberate rejection of truth, even in the face of undeniable evidence of God's power and presence in Jesus.

4: Trusting in God is rooted in knowing His character and Word. Fear and distrust arise from focusing on circumstances rather than God's promises.

5: Alexander the Coppersmith exemplifies the opposition faced by early Christian leaders. Paul's response—warning others while trusting God's ultimate justice—highlights the importance of discernment and reliance on divine judgment over personal retaliation.

6: Paul's exorcism of a demon-possessed slave girl, while demonstrating spiritual authority, led to unexpected consequences, demonstrating the complex interplay between spiritual power, economic interests, and societal reactions.

7: The miraculous healing of the crippled man in Lystra led to unexpected idolatry and misunderstanding, highlighting the challenges faced by Christian missionaries in communicating their message across cultural and religious barriers.

Free PDF
MAKE WISE DECISIONS

[Get the ebook version for 99 cents]

Consequences Shape Lives.

This book discusses the nature of decisions and explores eight essential questions to make better decisions.

You are a few decisions away from transforming your life. You can make better decisions! This resource has sections on what makes a poor decision, questions to ask yourself, traps to avoid, short and sweet decisions, the wise decision framework, and twenty ways to be wise. It also has a handy decision-making checklist. (12 pages)

Free PDF: https://getwisdompublishing.com/resource-registration/

Kindle ebook for 99 cents: https://www.amazon.com/dp/B0FG8NC53J

Ebook

Free PDF

Ten Steps to Wise Choices

Timeless Wisdom. Practical Tools. Lasting Impact.

Free PDF
Life Improvement Principles
[Get the ebook version for 99 cents]

You can live your best life!

Welcome to a journey of discovery! In case you have forgotten, your actions have consequences. Unlock your potential! This book (60+ pages) provides the overview of all our strategies and wisdom principles to live your best life. You *can* transform your life! Get your wisdom-based roadmap to a better life and unlock all the possibilities for growth and success.

Free PDF: https://getwisdompublishing.com/resource-registration/

Kindle ebook for 99 cents:
https://www.amazon.com/dp/B0FG883KZM

Ebook

Free PDF

Make it your life goal to be the best you can be!

Discover Wisdom and live the life you deserve.

Next Steps!

Continue Studying the *OBSCURE* Series
The *OBSCURE* Bible Study Series
https://www.amazon.com/dp/B08T7TL1B1

Be Challenged by the Jesus Follower Series
The Jesus Follower Bible Study Series
https://www.amazon.com/dp/B0DHP39P5J

Tackle Wisdom-Driven Life Change
Apply Biblical Wisdom to Live Your Best Life!
"Effective Life Change"
https://www.amazon.com/dp/1952359732

Know What You Should Pray
Personal Daily Prayer Guide
https://www.amazon.com/What-Should-Pray-Personal-Journal/dp/1952359260/

Decide to be the Very Best You Can Be
The Life Planning Series
https://www.amazon.com/dp/B09TH9SYC4

You Can Help:
SOCIAL MEDIA: Mention The *OBSCURE* Bible Study Series on your social platforms. Include the hashtag #obscurebiblestudy so we are aware of your post.

FRIENDS: Recommend *OBSCURE* to your family, friends, small group, Sunday School class leaders, or your church.

REVIEW: Please give us your honest review at
https://www.amazon.com/dp/1952359163

The *OBSCURE* Bible Study Series

Continue your journey through the hidden wisdom of Scripture with the OBSCURE Series.

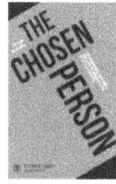

Blasphemy, Grace, Quarrels & Reconciliation: The lives of first-century disciples.
This book presents Joseph of Arimathea, Joanna, Ananias, Hymenaeus, and Cornelius (a centurion). It illustrates the nature and challenges of life as a first-century disciple.

The Beginning and the End: From creation to eternity.
This book has four lessons from Genesis and four from Revelation covering creation, rebellion, grace, worship, and eternity. God is leading us to worship in the Throne Room.

God at the Center: He is sovereign and I am not.
This book examines the virgin birth, worship, prayer, the sovereignty of God, compromise, and trust. God is at the center of all these stories. He is at the center of our lives.

Women of Courage: God did some serious business with these women.
This book examines the lives of Jael, Rizpah, the woman of Tekoa, Tabitha, Shiphrah, and Lydia. These women exhibit great courage and faithfulness. God used them in amazing ways.

The Beginning of Wisdom: Your personal character counts.
In this book we find courage, loyalty, thankfulness, love, forgiveness, and humility. Personal character counts. Decisions have consequences. Wisdom will help us stand firm in our faith.

Miracles & Rebellion: The good, the bad, and the indifferent.
God hates sin and loves to heal the faithful. The rebellion of Korah, Haman, and Alexander compare to the healing stories of Aeneas, a slave girl, and the crippled man at Lystra.

The Chosen People: There is a remnant.
This book concentrates mostly on Israel in the Old Testament, but also covers some interesting subjects as Lucifer, Michael the archangel, and Job's wife.

The Chosen Person: Keep your eyes on Jesus.
The focus is on Jesus and the superiority of Christ. We investigate Melchizedek, the disciples on the road to Emmaus, Nicodemus, and the criminal on the cross.

WEBSITE: http://getwisdompublishing.com/products/
AMAZON: www.amazon.com/author/stephenhberkey

Jesus Follower Bible Study Series

The Jesus Follower Bible Study Series will provide you with a complete description of the nature, characteristics, obligations, commitments, and responsibilities of a true Jesus follower.

Go to our Amazon Book Series page for your copy:

https://www.amazon.com/dp/B0DHP39P5J

The RELATIONSHIP CHARACTERISTICS of a Jesus Follower:
> Are you right with God?

The ONE ANOTHER INSTRUCTIONS to a Jesus Follower:
> Are you right with one another?

The WORSHIP of a Jesus Follower:
> Is your worship acceptable or in vain?

The PRAYER of a Jesus Follower:
> What Scripture says about unleashing the power of God.

The DANGERS of SIN for a Jesus Follower:
> God HATES sin! He abhors sin!

The FOCUS for a Jesus Follower:
> Keep your eyes fixed on Jesus!

The HEART Requirements of a Jesus Follower:
> Follow with all your heart, mind, body, and soul!

The COMMITMENTS of a Jesus Follower:
> Practical Christian living and discipleship.

The OBEDIENCE Requirements for a Jesus Follower:
> Ignore at your own risk!

"Get Wisdom Publishing creates wisdom-driven products that equip readers with timeless insights, understanding, and actionable tools to transform their lives."

Life Planning Series

Read these books if you want to live a better life.

The primary audience for this series is the secular self-help market, but the concepts are Christian based.

CHOOSE FAITH	**For the spiritual seeker and those with spiritual questions.** *Your Spiritual Guidebook For Questions About Religion, God, Heaven, Truth, Evil, and the Afterlife.* https://www.amazon.com/dp/1952359473
CHOOSE CORE VALUES	**Core values will drive your life.** https://www.amazon.com/dp/195235949X

Other Titles in the Life Planning Series
CHOOSE Integrity
CHOOSE Friends Wisely
CHOOSE The Right Words
CHOOSE Good Work Habits
CHOOSE Financial Responsibility
CHOOSE A Positive Self-Image
CHOOSE Leadership
CHOOSE Love and Family
LIFE PLANNING HANDBOOK A Life Plan Is The Key To Personal Growth https://www.amazon.com/gp/product/1952359325

Go to:

https://www.amazon.com/dp/B09TH9SYC4

to get these books.

Personal Daily Prayer Guide
Prayer Resource and Journal

This is a great resource to kick-start your prayer life!

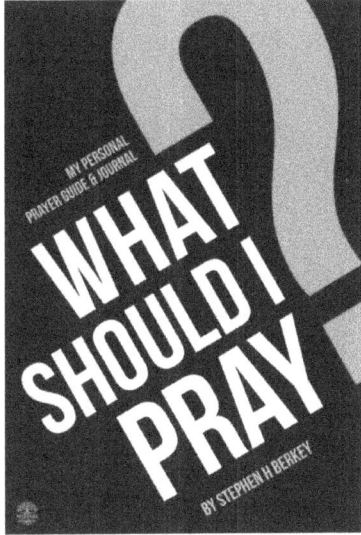

Know what to pray.
Pray based on Bible verses.
Strengthen your prayer life.
Access reference resources.
Pray with eternal implications.
Write your own prayers if desired.
Organize and focus your prayer time.
Learn what the Bible says about prayer.
Find encouragement and advice on how to pray.
Reduce frustration and distraction in your prayer time.

Get your copy today!

https://www.amazon.com/What-Should-Pray-Personal-Journal/dp/1952359260/

Acknowledgments

Arlene
Arlene has served as wife, editor, and proof-reader for all of my writing – thank you for your patience, help, and love.

Michelle
Michelle, our older daughter, has been an invaluable resource. She has graciously produced the website at www.getwisdompublishing.com. She was the first author in the family: graceandthegravelroad.com.

Stephanie
Our middle daughter designed all the covers for the *OBSCURE* Bible Study Series, as well as the marks and logos for Get Wisdom Publishing. We are grateful for her talent!

KOINONIA Small Group
These dear friends have hung in there with me as I taught many of the lessons to them first. Their input, answers, and suggestions have been invaluable.

God, Jesus, and Holy Spirit
Thank you, Lord, for Your guidance and direction.

Notes

1 Dana Chau, Sermon Central.com: https://www.sermoncentral.com/sermons/what-we-believe-mankind-part-3-dana-chau-sermon-on-becoming-a-christian-59512

2 Nelson's Illustrated Bible Dictionary, Copyright © 1986, Thomas Nelson Publishers; from PC Study Bible, "Propitiation"

3 Nelson's Illustrated Bible Dictionary, Copyright © 1986, Thomas Nelson Publishers; from PC Study Bible, "Forgiveness"

4 Nelson's Illustrated Bible Dictionary, Copyright © 1986, Thomas Nelson Publishers; from PC Study Bible, "Blasphemy"

5 The NIV Study Bible, New International Version, Zondervan Publishing House, © 1985, study notes on Acts 14:12

About the Author

Steve attended church as a child and accepted Christ when he was 10 years old. But his walk with Jesus left a lot to be desired for the next 44 years. In 1994 he "wrestled" with God for some period of months and in September of that year totally surrendered his life to Jesus.

In 1996 he was so driven to study God's Word that he attended the Indianapolis campus of Trinity Evangelical Divinity School (Chicago) to earn a Certificate of Biblical Studies. His hunger for God's Word led him to lead and write all his own Bible studies for his small group. He has been an entrepreneur and Bible study leader for the past 30 years.

He is a member of The Church at Station Hill in Spring Hill, TN, a regional campus of Brentwood Baptist (Brentwood TN).

GET**WISDOM**
P U B L I S H I N G

www.getwisdompublishing.com

"Get Wisdom Publishing is dedicated to being the trusted source of wisdom-driven books that inspire growth, guide decisions, and empower readers to live with purpose and fulfillment."

Contact Us

Website: www.getwisdompublishing.com

Email: info@getwisdompublishing.com

Facebook: Get Wisdom Publishing

Author's Page: www.amazon.com/author/stephenhberkey

Amazon's Obscure Bible Study Series page:
https://www.amazon.com/dp/B08T7TL1B1

"Go beyond devotionals.
Experience biblical wisdom in action!"